VANISHING
ANIMAL
NEIGHBORS

VANISHING ANIMAL NEIGHBORS

by Geraldine Marshall Gutfreund

Franklin Watts
New York / Chicago / London / Sydney
A First Book

Cover photograph courtesy of Todd Fink.
Photographs courtesy of: Cecil Schwalbe, 2, 20, 23, 24 (top &
left), 27; Todd Fink, 5, 6, 16, 53 (top & right), 56 (top); the Ohio
Department of Natural Resources (Alvin E. Staffan), 12, 15, 48, 56
(left); Tom Tyning, Massachusetts Audubon Society, 19 (left);
Mark Picard, 19 (right); Robert L. Nuhn, 28, 31 (top & right), 33,
34, 38 (top); Geraldine Marshall Gutfreund, 37, 38 (left), 42; the
Cincinnati Zoo and Botanical Garden (Ron Austing), 40, 46; U.S.
Fish & Wildlife Service, 45; Andy Sacks/Tony Stone Worldwide,
51; Tom McHugh/Photo Researchers, 55.

Library of Congress Cataloging-in-Publication Data

Gutfreund, Geraldine Marshall.
Vanishing animal neighbors/by Geraldine Marshall Gutfreund.
p.   cm.—(A First book)
Includes bibliographical references (p.   ) and index.
Summary: Describes the plight of such endangered animals as the
salamander, garter snake, and monarch butterfly.
ISBN 0-531-20060-4 (HC : library binding)
ISBN 0-531-15674-5   (paperback)
1. Endangered species—United States—Juvenile literature.
2. Wildlife conservation—United States—Juvenile literature.
[1. Rare animals. 2. Wildlife conservation.] I. Title.
II. Series.
QL84.2.G88 1993
591.52'9—dc20
92-25530 CIP AC

CONTENTS

ACKNOWLEDGMENTS

Many organizations and individuals gave their time in answering my requests for information. I want to thank the various state wildlife departments that sent state endangered species lists, information, and answered questions, especially Craig Stihler with the West Virginia Department of Natural Resources; Denis Case and Paul Schiff with the Ohio Department of Natural Resources; Cecil Schwalbe and Randy Babb with the Arizona Game and Fish Department; Todd Fink and Deanna Glosser with the Illinois Department of Conservation; Michelle Martin with the Indiana Department of Natural Resources; Paul Moler with the Florida Game and Freshwater Fish Commission; Paul Kelly of the California Department of Fish and Game; and John Albright with the Maine Natural Heritage Program. I also want to thank the U.S. Fish and Wildlife Service; the World Wildlife Fund, especially Michael O'Connell; the Animal Welfare Institute; the Nature Conservancy, especially Catherine Heller with the California field office and Marleen Kromer with the Ohio Chapter; the New Jersey Wildlife Preservation Trust; the Texas Organization for Endangered Species; the Center for Environmental Information, Inc.; the Office of Migratory Bird Management, especially John Trapp; the International Council for Bird Preservation; the Manomet Bird Observatory; the Audubon Society, especially Barbara Linton; the Xerces Society; the Cincinnati Zoo, especially Dawn Strasser and Leslie Lorrance; Carol Burke with *Wildlife Conservation* magazine; David Wake; Thomas Emmel; Douglas Sutherland with the Entomological Society of America; and Tom Borgman, Penny Borgman, and Bob Nuhn with the Hamilton County Park District. As usual, the help of the Public Library of Cincinnati and Hamilton County, especially of the Mt. Healthy Branch, was invaluable. Special thanks to Nancy Jones Hamson for lending me her many conservation magazines. Once again, the support of the members of my writers' group—Teresa Cleary, Linda Kleinschmidt, Andrea Rotterman, and Jean Syed—kept me writing. Thanks to my editor, Mary Perrotta Rich, for suggesting a book on endangered animals. Thanks to Tigger Harper—and his mistress, Karen—for domestic housecat measurements. Thanks to my family just for being there, and especially to my daughters, Audrey and Rachel, who are a constant reminder of the magic of all life.

The Great Magician of Planet Earth

You are watching The Great Magician of Planet Earth perform. "Watch me pull a rabbit out of the hat," the magician says. Out of the hat comes a large white rabbit. "Now watch the rabbit disappear." The rabbit disappears, but you know that in the next performance the rabbit will be back.

"Now," says the magician, "Go back in time with me to the year 1850." With a wave of the wand, millions of birds darken the sky like an eclipse of the sun. There is the sound that an American Indian chief described as "a gurgling, rumbling sound, as though an army of horses jangling sleigh bells was advancing...." You are watching a migration of one of the most numerous birds that ever lived, passenger pigeons. But when the cloud of birds disappears into The Great Magician's hat, not even one can be pulled back out. Passenger pigeons have disappeared from the Earth forever. They are extinct, and no magic can make them reappear.

When a type of animal, a species or subspecies, becomes extinct, there are none of that type of animal left alive. Scientists know that for millions of years many species of animals have become naturally extinct because of physical changes in their environment. The changes can be in the climate or they can be changes in the type of animals and plants that live with them, such as the invasion of a competitor for their food.

But today, humans are the reason that many animals are disappearing before they would naturally become extinct. No one is sure how many animal species are being lost, but some scientists estimate that at least three species are becoming extinct each day.

Animal species are vanishing because the animals' habitats—their homes—are being polluted, changed, and destroyed. Michael O'Connell, a biologist with the World Wildlife Fund, says that "the majority of problems with endangered species begins with habitat loss."

Animal species are also vanishing because people kill or collect too many of them for food, for sport, as pets, or for the resources that they provide, such as oil, feathers, ivory, etc. Species are vanishing because people bring new animals into the native animals' habitat. This may cause competition for available food or even cause the native animals to become a food source for the new animals.

There are many reasons to save endangered species. All animals have value. Some are valued for their beauty, others for their usefulness as food or other products. Yet others are necessary as food for other species. Often we are not sure what purpose a species might be serving in its environment until it is gone. Most importantly, all species have value just because they are themselves. A great man who cared for all life, Dr. Albert Schweitzer, said, "Animals and plants are our brothers and sisters, and we are beholden to look after them."

Few people believed that the many-numbered passenger pigeon would ever become extinct. But a combination of overhunting and habitat loss caused the world to lose forever these birds with dawn-pink breasts that filled the sky with the sound of sleigh bells.

This book is about vanishing animal neighbors in the United States. Watch The Great Magician pull out salamanders, monarch butterflies, songbirds, garter snakes, and jaguarundis. Learn why these animals are vanishing, what is being done to save them, and how you can help so that they do not disappear forever.

CHAPTER ONE

Salamanders

Disappearing Buried Treasure

On a cold, February night, a group of people gathers together for a treasure hunt. We are going into the woods of our local park to search for Jefferson salamanders.

Some of the kids in our group have brought buckets. "No taking salamanders," says Penny Borgman, the park naturalist. She tells us that

Jefferson salamanders spend most of the year burrowed beneath the ground and are rarely seen. But in early spring they breed in shallow ponds.

Jefferson salamanders are one of about 350 species of salamanders ranging in size from an Asian salamander almost as long as a man is tall, to a Mexican salamander no larger than your little finger. Unlike their cousins the frogs and toads, salamanders are usually silent. Most live in cool, shady places, often under rocks and leaves or in the ground. They are mostly nocturnal, or active at night. Salamanders are often literally right beneath our feet without our knowing it.

In some forests of eastern North America, scientists estimate that if all of the salamanders were weighed, they would weigh more than all of the birds and mammals put together. This many animals found together tells scientists that salamanders are important to the forests, as food for other animals, as predators of insects, slugs, snails, and worms, and possibly for other undiscovered reasons.

Jefferson salamanders belong to a group of salamanders known as mole salamanders because they spend most of their lives underground as moles do.

Salamanders can be brown and sprinkled with silver-blue specks (as is the Jefferson salamander), bright orange or green, and many other colors. Some even are striped like miniature tigers.

13

We reach a small pond. A dozen flashlights reflect against the dark surface of the water. In the pond is our hidden treasure. First we see masses of salamander eggs in a protective jelly, looking like bunches of grapes clinging to low branches and dipping into the pond. Then we notice the brownish salamanders in traps that were set earlier in the day so we would be able to get a good look at these secretive amphibians.

Penny gives us a better look at these salamander treasures, which she will then return to the pond. She passes around one salamander in a plastic petri dish so that we can look carefully without harming the salamander's moist skin. Then it is time for us, and for the salamanders, to go home.

But in many parts of North America, salamanders are in danger of losing their homes—and their lives. The frightening fact is that during the past ten years, scientists all around the world have noticed a decline in many species of amphibians, including salamanders. Dr. David Wake, who studies amphibians, says that he is especially concerned "that widespread, supposedly common ['safe'] species are in decline and now in trouble."

The clearest reasons that salamanders are vanishing is the destruction of their habitats by humans. People use the land for houses, farms,

Tiger salamanders are found throughout much of North America from southern Canada to southern Mexico, but are now endangered in certain areas. Also mole salamanders, they spend much of the year underground and are generally seen in the late winter/early spring breeding season.

businesses, and roads. The Jefferson salamander is considered rare in a number of states, including Massachusetts. The Massachusetts Natural Heritage Program says that, "The major threat to this species . . . is the loss of wetland habitat."

A number of salamanders are threatened by logging. The Red Hills salamander, found only in Alabama, has lost much of its home to logging for wood that is used to make paper. The Cheat Mountain salamander is found only in West Virginia. Logging, as well as mines and roads that

Marbled salamanders are threatened in Massachusetts because of habitat loss from land development, acid rain, pesticide spraying, and from being run over when they cross busy roads to reach breeding areas.

the salamanders can't cross, has destroyed much of its habitat.

Sometimes the destruction of salamander homes occurs for surprising reasons. The California Department of Fish and Game lists the limestone salamander as a threatened species. Its most serious threat is a proposed gold mine!

There is hope for salamanders whose clear threat is habitat destruction. Government agencies, as well as private organizations, can sometimes buy and protect land for rare species.

Preserves, however, are only a first step. Often it takes a very large area to allow animals to live and breed. Even if the land is saved, there is still danger in both protected and unprotected areas of what scientists call degradation of habitat. This means that the habitat is changed in a negative way. Many things can degrade a habitat.

Salamanders are threatened by many kinds of pollution. All amphibians have moist skin that absorbs the gases and liquids around them. Some salamanders breath mainly through their skin. So along with gases such as oxygen that they need to live, amphibians' skins also absorb many kinds of pollution. Because they live both on land and in water they absorb both land and water pollution.

Pesticides are believed to have harmed several populations of salamanders, including Jefferson and marbled salamanders. Acid rain, caused by the burning of coal and oil that releases chemicals into the air that then combine with moisture to form acidic rain, snow, and fog, could also be harming salamanders. Studies of tiger salamanders show that in the Colorado Rocky Mountains, the acidity of the snow that melts into the breeding ponds was high at the time the eggs were developing. Other studies of amphibian eggs have shown that when the acidity of water increases, as many as one-fourth to one-third of eggs don't hatch. Those eggs that do hatch may produce deformed animals.

Scientists also wonder if recent suspected changes in the earth's climate (global warming) and the decrease in the ozone layer because of pollutants could be affecting amphibians.

Dr. Wake says, "In short, amphibian decline is a message." It's a message that too many things are being done that harm our Earth.

People are trying to help salamanders. In some cities, people have closed roads during the time salamanders are migrating across roads to get to breeding ponds. In Amherst, Massachusetts, people have even built a special tunnel under the road for migrating spotted salamanders. A twelve-year-old boy helped save a wetland by organizing his community to protest condominium development that would have destroyed a number of species, including blue-spotted salamanders. Kids in New Jersey have formed a group called Kids Against Pollution to help solve the problems of pollution. John Albright, director of the Natural Heritage Program in Maine, says that, "Kids are really good at looking at things such as salamanders. They should learn to be good caretakers of our common species by increasing awareness in adults of what exists." Kids can write letters to those who destroy habitats and cause pollution, invite biologists to

(left) These people are building a special salamander tunnel under Henry Street in Amherst, Massachusetts to help spotted salamaders safely cross. Around late March, spotted salamanders leave their underground homes and migrate to breeding pools. Hundreds of salamanders are killed by traffic each year during their spring migration.

(below) Thanks to the salamander tunnel, this spotted salamander is safely on its way to a breeding pool.

come and talk to their classes, and even put a sign up. "Here's a breeding site. Stay away."

In the Appalachian Mountains, people once believed that each spring system had a salamander that kept the water clean and healthy. If the salamander was disturbed and disappeared, the springs would dry up. Salamanders are a magic we don't want to lose.

Garter Snakes

Striped Scarves Fading from the Magician's Pockets

In the reptile house at the Cincinnati Zoo there are what some people think are the most beautiful snakes in our country: San Francisco garter snakes.

A bright yellow-green stripe runs down each snake's back, banded by black and red stripes to the sides. We glimpse turquoise blue bellies. They remind us of bright, magic scarves that The Great

Magician might mysteriously pull from a pocket. What fun it would be to travel to California, stand by a pond in a summer meadow, and watch such snakes in the wild. But the Vanishing Animal symbol on the display sign shows that San Francisco garter snakes could vanish from their few pockets of the Earth like the Magician's Scarves.

Found around and just south of the San Francisco Bay area of California, San Francisco garter snakes live near ponds, marshes, and slow-moving streams. They like water with lots of surrounding plants where they can feed on their favorite food, red-legged frogs. They like to live near hillsides where they can bask in the sun and have rodent burrows to hide in.

Once, such wetlands and hillsides were easily available to San Francisco garter snakes. Then many people settled in the area. These people changed the land. They built homes, industries, and roads. They made farms and ranches. They brought in cattle. Cattle eat the plants that grow around the water, and fewer frogs can survive without this plant growth. The San Francisco garter snakes lost their homes and their food.

Unlike some snakes, garter snakes do not lay eggs, but give birth to live young. San Francisco garter snakes give birth in July and August to between three and eighty-five live young. The U.S. Fish and Wildlife Service lists San Francisco garter snakes as endangered.

Those that remain in pockets of habitat are in danger of being trampled by people on golf courses and by cattle on ranches, harmed by chemicals applied to control weeds, and run over by cars. The snakes are further endangered by reptile dealers and collectors who illegally capture them to sell or for collections.

Nearby in Arizona and Mexico, both the narrow-headed and Mexican garter snakes may be in danger of disappearing. One reason Mexican garter snakes are in danger is surprising. You know snakes eat frogs, but did you know frogs eat snakes?

At the beginning of the century, bullfrogs were brought in and released in wetlands for people who wanted to dine on frog-leg dinners. The bullfrogs multiplied in their new home. Randy Babb, a biologist with the Arizona Game and Fish Department, reports that during the summer rainy season, bullfrogs can go right across the desert and reach new bodies of water. The biologists have discovered that the bullfrogs eat young garter snakes. The bullfrogs even eat some adult garter snakes, as grown garter snakes have been found in the stomachs of bullfrogs. Biologists are trying to control the numbers of bullfrogs, and the garter snake population seems to be increasing.

This Mexican garter snake's tail has probably been bitten by a bullfrog. Mexican garter snakes eat small rodents, fish, earthworms, and frogs.

Humans have also introduced non-native bass and other fish for sport fishing. Those fish are a danger to both narrow-headed and Mexican garter snakes. Not only do the bass eat the smaller fish and tadpoles that the garter snakes eat, they, too, may eat young garter snakes.

But the main reason that these garter snakes are in danger is that their habitats are being destroyed. The marshlands, called "lands of a thou-

(above): The Verde River at Camp Verde, Arizona still provides good wetland habitat for Mexican garter snakes. A journal from the early 1800's reports that as many as 200 beavers were sometimes caught in a night. Beavers helped raise the groundwater tables by damming streams, helping to provide the habitat these snakes need.

(left): This former Mexican garter snake habitat formed by the Gila River, south of Phoenix, Arizona, shows modern day threats to Mexican garter snakes. The brown streak across the sky is polluted air.

sand waters," where Mexican garter snakes live, are decreasing. The wetlands are currently being destroyed by the pumping of their water to supply agriculture, homes, and industries. Other things, such as cattle grazing, also hurt the wetlands. Some of the streams and small rivers where narrow-headed garter snakes live, have been dammed. "If we lose those habitats," says Randy Babb, "we lose those snakes."

This is also true in Ohio where eastern plains garter snakes are endangered. These brightly striped garter snakes live in tall grass prairies. More than ninety percent of Ohio's prairies have been destroyed by farms. Denis Case, a biologist with the Ohio Department of Natural Resources, points out that, "Eastern plains garter snakes have served as an index of the disappearance of the prairies. Had someone been monitoring the eastern plains garter snakes sooner, we would have been aware sooner of the disappearance of the prairies." Only one population of eastern plains garter snakes is left in Ohio. He says that many species have disappeared or are disappearing with the prairies, such as greater prairie chickens and bison.

People in federal and state wildlife agencies and private conservation organizations are trying to preserve land for all of these endangered garter snakes. Sometimes, plans are made to recreate habitat that has been lost. Some areas where San Francisco garter snakes live are fenced off to prevent people and cars from trampling the snakes and to keep people from collecting them. It is hoped that programs can be developed in some of the state parks to tell people about San Francisco garter snakes so that people will be careful to protect the snakes.

Even small things can make a difference. On the protected tall grass prairie in Ohio where the eastern plains garter snakes live, it was found that when areas were mowed to keep the grasslands from being taken over by other types of plants, snakes were being chopped up by the mowers. By studying the snakes, people found that during the hottest part of the day, the snakes burrow into the crayfish burrows where they are safe from mowers. Now the mowing is done during the hottest part of the day. The people mowing may be hot, but they are saving endangered snakes!

The Fish and Wildlife Service says garter snakes are helpful because they prey on other animals such as mice. Denis Case says garter snakes are food for birds of prey, but more important, they are "part of the natural system, the same system we're in, so the healthier they are, the healthier we are."

Biologists are concerned about Mexican garter snakes in Arizona and New Mexico where habitat has been lost. Mexican garter snakes are also found in the country of Mexico. Garter snakes are named after the fancy, striped bands called garters that were once used to hold up men's socks.

Watching the San Francisco garter snakes, we know that we should not take for granted the common eastern garter snake that lives in our woods. Even commonly found garter snakes have become less populous in areas with heavy development. We want to continue to be amazed by beautiful garter snakes appearing from many pockets.

CHAPTER THREE

Monarch Butterflies

Migrating Magic
Going, Going...

"Hear," says The Great Magician of Planet Earth, "how monarch butterflies came to be."

"As daylight was closing one autumn day, the Creator was walking the earth and wishing that colors might truly be alive. So the Creator took from the sunset a spoon of orange, veined by dark shadows of tree branches. Then, to the delight of gathering children, from the Creator's hands flew a butterfly. The butterfly made of sunset and shadows was the monarch butterfly.

"But in the morning the monarch flew far away to where winter wouldn't rule. 'Wait!' cried the children, 'come back!'

"The monarch must migrate to live through the cold winter,' said the Creator, 'but your friend will return in the spring when the milkweed plants grow again.' And so, each spring the monarch does return."

This story of the monarch butterfly's creation makes an imporant point: North American monarchs migrate in the late summer and autumn to where they can survive the winter. They then return in the spring to lay their eggs on milkweed plants.

Monarchs are named for the rulers of kingdoms, such as kings or queens. Early English settlers named the splendid butterflies after King William. Monarchs are sometimes called King Billy butterflies.

North American monarchs are the only insects that scientists are sure migrate south to the same places every year to overwinter and then return north every year. What is even more amazing is that the monarchs who return south to the wintering grounds each year are at least the great-great-great-grandchildren of those who came north in the spring.

29

There are two groups of monarchs in North America. One group lives during warm weather in the valleys of the Rocky Mountains and overwinters along the coast of California. From one to five million monarchs winter in California. The other group lives during warm weather east of the Rocky Mountains. These monarchs migrate mainly to the mountains of Mexico. On their overwintering grounds the monarchs live huddled together on fir trees in Mexico, and on oak, sycamore, alder, gum, and palm trees in California. They look like butterfly trees! The monarchs live in a sleepy state, sipping little nectar, and only drinking and flying occasionally.

Bob Nuhn, an Ohio park ranger, traveled to Mexico to see the monarchs. He says, "The first thing I saw was these trees looking like beehives, dark masses that reminded me of bee swarms. The butterflies were weighing down the boughs of these fir branches—hundreds of thousands of butterflies all in one spot. In the space of a hand, [there were] a hundred butterflies."

Bob explains that the butterflies can't fly often or they'll use up their body fat and starve before returning to North America in the spring. But they must fly sometimes or their wing muscles will become weak. "The next thing I noticed was that

(above) Scientists are not sure how the monarchs know how to reach their wintering grounds. They may use the position of the sun or the earth's magnetic field to guide them. The overwintering sites form a circle around a mine that gives high magnetic readings and monarchs have been found to have magnetite, a mineral also found in the bodies of pigeons and dolphins. The butterflies might be drawn to the sites as though to a magnet.

(right) The butterflies at an overwintering site are known as a colony.

when the sun came out I saw hundreds of thousands of monarchs flying in the sky. They were like orange leaves that never end, or like millions of tiny orange kites. There were so many, you could hear a fluttering in the air like somebody lightly turning the pages of paper all around you. It wasn't until the end of the day that I thought I should've enjoyed it more because I realized I'd never get to see it again."

North American monarch butterflies are in danger of losing their winter homes in Mexico and California. If this happens, they will not be able to return to their summer homes throughout the United States and on into Canada. In most parts of the United States and Canada, monarchs would be gone forever.

The fir forests in Mexico are being cut down by logging and for farms. The monarchs depend on very specific temperatures in their semidormant overwintering states. Even small cuttings in the fir forests can cause the temperature to drop to a point low enough to kill the butterflies.

In California, winter roosting sites are being turned into developments. Other threats in California are chemicals used to fertilize plants and to kill insects and weeds. The butterflies drink poisonous water from lawns treated with chemicals.

This male monarch, drinking nectar from swamp milkweed in August, is storing energy for its long migration to Mexico. Monarchs may fly as far as 80 miles (129 kilometers) in a day.

Some scientists are concerned that modern agriculture is reducing the amounts and kinds of milkweed and other wildflowers growing in fields and along roadsides. The monarch caterpillars feed only on milkweed, and the adult butterflies need nectar from both milkweed and other flowers to provide fuel for their long migration. Some milkweeds contain a poisonous substance that does not hurt monarchs, but does make them distasteful to predatory birds. When the caterpillars eat the milk-

Looking like millions of tiny orange kites winging in the wind, monarchs fly occasionally at the overwintering sites to keep their wings in shape. They cannot fly too often or they will use up their fat reserves and starve.

weeds, they store this substance, which stays with them when they become adults. This is a natural protection. Some scientists think that the poisonous milkweeds are now decreasing, making monarchs more vulnerable to birds.

Though monarch butterflies are not endangered as a species because they exist in a number of places in the world, the two-way migration behavior of the North American monarch butterflies is considered by scientists to be an endangered phenomenon. A phenomenon is a rare and spectacular event. The monarchs that live year round in other places, mostly in warm, tropical countries, are not known to perform the same spectacular migration behavior that the North American monarchs do. If the North American monarchs' winter habitats are destroyed, not only will the butterfly of sunset and shadows vanish from our summer gardens, a fantastic event of the animal world will also disappear.

But, this may not have to happen. The president of Mexico issued a promise to protect the monarch's overwintering sites, and created a reserve to protect several areas. Logging and agricultural development have been prohibited or restricted on 40,000 acres. In California, Pacific

Grove, nicknamed "Butterfly Town U.S.A.," recently voted to set aside a habitat area where the butterflies overwinter. Conservation groups such as the Xerces Society, the World Wildlife Fund, and a Mexican group of naturalists, Monarca A.C., are working to preserve overwintering sites.

Some people helping to save the monarch are involved in the Monarch for National Insect campaign. Dr. Douglas Sutherland, a scientist involved with the campaign, says that "this campaign is not only to save monarchs, but to allow the monarch to serve as a representative of insects, to draw attention to some 90,000 insects in the United States—the vast majority of which are beneficial"—and a number of which are endangered.

Dr. Sutherland suggests that kids can help the monarchs by writing their senators and representatives and sending pictures supporting the monarchs for national insect and preserving monarchs' and other insects' habitats.

Another thing you can do is plant a butterfly garden, a garden of plants that provides nectar for butterflies as well as food for their caterpillars.

If you're lucky enough to have milkweeds in your yard, leave them for the monarchs. Your parents might not want their milkweed plants, but

As part of a Girl Scout troop project, these girls are writing letters to their senator asking support for the Monarch for National Insect campaign. They've also started seeds for a butterfly garden.

(above) This monarch butterfly caterpillar is on the leaf of a common milkweed plant. Monarchs lay eggs on the underside of milkweed leaves. The larva, or caterpillar, emerges in about four or five days. The caterpillar feeds on milkweed and grows for two to three weeks. The caterpillar next becomes pupa, also called a chrysalis. In about nine to fifteen days after the pupa forms, the adult monarch butterfly will be ready to emerge.

(left) Milkweed pods in fall. You can collect the brown seeds to plant for monarchs.

you might be able to move them to a special spot. Try collecting milkweed seeds in the fall. You can then plant the seeds in the fall. You might also experiment with planting in the spring. Dr. Sutherland suggests storing the seeds in a plastic bag in the refrigerator, possibly with some powdered milk to absorb moisture. Plant some directly outside after the last freeze, or start them indoors first in the spring and transplant the seedlings outdoors.

The monarchs need a lot of nectar to store up body fat to live through the winter. They feed little if at all in the winter or there would not be enough nectar for the millions of butterflies that need it. About one-third of the body weight of migrating monarchs is fat.

For monarchs and other butterflies, try planting one or more of these nectar sources: black-eyed susans, phlox, impatiens, marigolds, daisies, cosmos, and zinnias. Pick a sunny, sheltered spot. Provide some water for visiting butterflies by putting a few stones in a shallow tray and filling it with water.

Your plants could help one of nature's greatest magic shows keep going.

CHAPTER FOUR

Jaguarundis

Cats Playing Hide and Seek with Survival

Outside the Cincinnati Zoo's nursery, a pink and blue sign announces the recent birth of two jaguarundi kittens, a black male and a red female. Inside the nursery, the five-week-old kittens are behaving like "true kittens," says Dawn Strasser, the nursery keeper.

"They really enjoy their toys," Dawn says. The kittens' toys include a squeaking, yellow Big Bird and a large pink ball. "They get on top and balance themselves on the ball. Then they'll do somer-saults, hanging on the ball as it goes around."

Dawn hands me the female kitten who tumbles as playfully in my lap as a domestic kitten might. Weighing 1.45 pounds (663 grams), she is not much bigger than a five-week-old domestic kitten. She will only grow to between 12 and 22 pounds (5.4 to 9.9 kg), about the weight of a large house cat. She will, though, grow to about 41 to 55 inches (104 to 140 cm) long, a foot or two longer than the average house cat. As much as two feet of her length will be her long tail.

The jaguarundis stay a lot closer to the ground than other cats. Being good swimmers and having a long, low-slung shape have earned jaguarundis the nickname "otter cats." Their shape helps them move quickly through the thick brush areas where they usually live and hunt mostly birds. Jaguarundis range from southern Texas and possibly southern Arizona, south into Mexico, Central, and South America.

Much as we keep domestic cats today, jaguarundis are believed to have been tamed and kept by early natives to keep their villages free of mice and rats. Many people today who report seeing jaguar-undis may have instead seen house cats.

Kittens from the same litter can range in color from black to gray to red, just as children born to the same parents can have different hair colors. It was once thought that the red jaguarundis were a separate species. The red jaguarundis were called eyra cats. Now scientists know that the cats all belong to the same species.

Dawn puts the kitten back with its brother, and we turn away for a moment. A repeated birdlike chirping is heard in the nursery. The sound is coming from the jaguarundi kitten! Jaguarundis also make purring and coughing sounds.

When we leave the jaguarundi kittens, they are playing with each other in what looks like hide and seek. Unfortunately, jaguarundis in the wild are also playing hide and seek with scientists who want to learn about them to help them survive.

Two subspecies of jaguarundis have been known to live in the United States. Both subspecies are endangered. Scientists do not know how many jaguarundis still live in the United States. In Arizona, biologist Randy Babb says that reliable sources still report seeing jaguarundis. "But," he adds, "no one has been able to take a photo or even get a long look to be sure."

Scientists in Texas are having the same problem finding proof of jaguarundis. Dr. Mike Tewes studies both jaguarundis and their cousins, ocelots. Ocelots live in the same areas and habitat as jaguarundis and are also in danger of becoming extinct in the United States. Dr. Tewes tries to trap the cats so that he can put radio collars on them, release them, and track them. To develop plans to preserve habitats, scientists need to know where the animals range. Ocelots have been trapped and released, but Dr. Tewes says jaguarundis "are a lot more secretive and a lot more clever at avoiding traps." Frank Goodwyn, a biologist who studied jaguarundis in the wild for two years, states that he never saw one! But in 1986, a jaguarundi was discovered in Texas. It had been run over by a car. Reports continue of jaguarundi sightings—some people even report seeing jaguarundis in their own backyards.

These sightings, tracks found in areas jaguarundis would live in, and the jaguarundi found killed by a car, lead scientists to believe the jaguarundis are still living in the United States. But true to another of their nicknames, ghost cat, jaguarundis slip through scientists' fingers as easily as a ghost.

It is easier to see the reasons why the last few jaguarundis are in danger of becoming extinct in the United States. The greatest threat to jaguarundis and ocelots is habitat destruction. The brushland where these cats live is being cleared for farms and pastures. When Dr. Tewes surveyed a thirteen county area of southern Texas, he reported that only one percent remained that was ideal ocelot and jaguarundi habitat.

Both of these pictures from the Santa Ana/ Rio Grande Valley National Wildlife refuges in Texas show jaguarundi habitat. Jaguarundis need a variety of habitats in order to survive. The silver-gray strands hanging from the trees (bottom picture) are Spanish moss.

Bird-like chirps, coughs, and purrs are common sounds that jaguarundis make. Scientists have discovered that jaguarundis make thirteen different calls. Jaguarundis are generally considered to be solitary animals, but some scientists suggest that this wide range of calls might mean that jaguarundis "talk" to each other about many things and are more social than previously believed.

People are trying to preserve enough land for the cats to remain in the United States. Refuges in Texas, such as the National Audubon Society's Sabal Palm Grove Sanctuary and the Nature Conservancy's Zamora Ben Preserve, are a start.

The U. S. Fish and Wildlife Service manages three refuges, the Laguna Tascosa National Wildlife Refuge, the Lower Rio Grande Valley National Wildlife Refuge, and the Santa Ana National Wildlife Refuge.

The Fish and Wildlife Service hopes to protect another 81,758 acres of land now owned by private landowners to preserve both blocks of habitats along with what are called wildlife corridors, smaller strips of land left undeveloped that the cats can use to travel to other safe areas. They could be called wildlife hallways, strips of wild land through developed land where jaguarundis, ocelots, and more than 115 other species of animals can walk free. Let's hope that these hallways can prevent the ghost cat from performing a final vanishing act.

CHAPTER FIVE

Songbirds
Fewer Musicians
to Play

Today has been a magic May day. Visitors to the woods can hear the clear ringing notes of a Kentucky warbler in the morning and the beautiful song of a wood thrush at dusk.

Though we love the cardinals and chickadees that stay with us through the winter, we are always happy to welcome back those songbirds that migrate south for the winter to Mexico, Belize, Costa Rica, Panama, Puerto Rico, and on into South America. Scientists call the about two hundred and fifty birds that migrate beyond the United States long-distance migrants, or Neotropical migrants, because the countries they migrate to are known as the Neotropics. In the spring they return to the United States, mostly to eastern forests, to build nests and raise chicks.

These returning songbirds are the voice of spring. Spring could be called the greatest magic show of the planet Earth, and these special song-birds provide the music for the show.

But many bird-watchers and scientists are now reporting that in many areas there are fewer and fewer Neotropical migrants. One study has shown that in the last ten years, wood thrush populations in the United States have gone down about 30 percent, almost one-third of their population.

This wood thrush is nesting in a hemlock tree. The wood thrush's song sounds like an enchanted flute and makes the woods a magic place.

Scientist Noble Proctor wrote in *Songbirds* that red-eyed vireos were once "the most commonly seen songbird of the eastern forest, but may become a rarity within the next few decades."

Scientist John Terborgh, writes in his book *Where Have All the Birds Gone?*

that the wood thrush, worm-eating warbler, Kentucky warbler, and hooded warbler "are species that face severe problems in the future. . . ."

Michael O'Connell, a biologist with the World Wildlife Fund, says, "Out of sixty-two migrant songbirds studied in the eastern United States, forty-four had population declines in the last ten years." He says, "This is a real problem. It's not a short-term problem that could be attributed to something that will just go away."

What is happening to warblers, vireos, thrushes, and other Neotropical migrants? They are losing both their summer and their winter homes.

In their summer homes in the United States (and Canada), the songbirds breed and raise their families. Early settlers in the United States said that a squirrel could go all the way from the Atlantic Ocean to the Mississippi River and its feet would never have to touch the ground. How far do you think that squirrel would get today without having to run across highways and parking lots? Not far. According to John Terborgh, "More than 99 percent of what the colonists found has been felled." Even though some land has been allowed to return to forest, there is much less habitat altogether. Those patches of forest that are left are essentially islands, although instead of being surrounded by

While we need farms to provide food for people, we also need forests and the variety of other habitats that provide homes and food for animals. We must plan carefully how we use land and other resources in order to preserve and provide for all in the future.

water, these forest islands are surrounded by plowed fields, roads, and shopping malls.

Many migrant songbirds do not live, breed, or raise their families successfully in these forest islands. First, the migrants, after traveling long distances, must find a mate and a place to breed in the same area. As the wooded regions become farther and farther apart, they are less likely to find a mate and a home before starving or being eaten!

Even reaching the forest islands can be difficult. Backyard trees, as well as larger areas, can be important stopovers for migrating birds. With more and more resting spots disappearing, the birds' problem has been compared to a game of musical chairs—with the chairs rapidly disappearing!

Even if a pair of songbirds is successful in nesting, there are many dangers to their eggs and chicks. Animals that prey on songbird eggs and young, such as blue jays, crows, and especially raccoons, thrive in woods surrounding the fields and suburbs. Domestic cats and dogs also prey on songbirds and their young.

Another important danger is that of cowbirds. Named cowbirds because they followed bison and other grazing animals about and ate the insects that were stirred up by the grazers, cowbirds were once birds of the Great Plains. Now, as the forests have been cleared and fields of food and domestic cattle are found throughout the eastern United States as well as Canada, the cowbirds have followed.

Cowbirds are a danger because they are nest parasites—they lay their eggs in other birds' nests. Cowbird chicks are large and they are greedy! Not

(above) This common yellowthroat (a warbler) is feeding a large cowbird chick, along with her own fledglings.

(right) This wood thrush's nest contains three blue thrush eggs and two cowbird eggs. Cowbirds are just one of the problems contributing to the decline of Neotropical migrants.

only do they sometimes trample the natural nestlings, they demand most of the food from the parents, who cannot tell their chicks from the cowbird chicks. The natural chicks often starve. A study in Illinois recently showed that out of fifteen wood thrush nests, only one wood thrush hatched and lived, but eight cowbirds flew away from those nests!

Although there are many problems with the migrant songbirds' summer homes, some scientists feel that the biggest problem is the loss of their tropical winter homes. Tropical forests are being rapidly cut down for farms, cattle pastures, and sugarcane fields. In Mexico alone, a Mexican biologist estimates that 247 acres (99.96 hectares) of rain forest are being cleared each day. This is as large an area as large as 187 football fields!

Still, there is hope for Neotropical songbirds. Scientific and conservation organizations are doing studies in Mexico, Central America, and South America to find out more about the needs of Neotropical migrants. They are looking for information such as how small a habitat area the birds can survive in. Researchers have found that some very profitable crops, such as coffee, mangos, and citrus fruits, can serve as good habitats for some

Once a rain forest and winter home for songbirds, this land in Mexico has been cleared for cattle grazing. People need to conserve as much natural habitat as possible and learn to use land wisely. There are ways to use land for both animals and people. Crops, such as coffee, mangos, and citrus fruits, can provide money and food for people and habitat for birds.

(above) Kentucky warblers are found not only in Kentucky, but in other states as well. Kentucky warblers often wag their tails as they walk and have been called Kentucky wagtails.

(left) The red-eyed vireo is one of The Great Magician's hardest working musicians. An almost constant singer, it has been reported to have sung 22,197 songs in one day. The red-eyed vireo in this picture is feeding a young cowbird.

migrants while providing people with a way to make a living.

Just by being aware of migratory songbirds, you can begin to make a difference. If it's your job to take out the garbage, help discourage raccoons, the major songbird predator, from making their homes near yours. Make sure the garbage can lid is on tight and raccoon-proof—tied if necessary.

Barbara Linton of the National Audubon Society suggests that kids encourage parents to leave even small undeveloped areas wild.

Students at a school in Cincinnati recently got together and collected enough money to contribute to a program that buys rain forest habitat to preserve it.

It's important that we keep both summer and winter homes for songbirds. Michael O'Connell says, "Even if a forest looks healthy, if songbirds are disappearing, something is wrong." The Great Magician would say that if we lose songbirds, the music will vanish from the magic show of life.

GLOSSARY

Acid rain—the acidic rain, snow, and fog formed when sulfur dioxide and nitrogen oxides are released into the air (through the burning of coal and oil) and combine with moisture in the air.

Amphibians—animals that include frogs and toads, salamanders, and caecilians (legless, wormlike animals) with smooth moist skin. Most, but not all, amphibians live both in water and on land.

Eclipse—when a planet, moon, or sun vanishes from view because the shadow of another planet or moon has obscured it.

Endangered species—a species of animal (or plant) that is in danger right now of becoming extinct in all of or a large part of the areas in which it lives.

Extinct—when no individuals of a type of animal (or plant) are alive.

Global warming—the possibility that the earth is getting warmer because people are burning fuels, cutting forests, etc., causing gases that trap heat, such as carbon dioxide, to increase.

Habitat—the place where an animal (or plant) lives.

Insects—animals without backbones with three body parts, six legs, and usually two pairs of wings.

Mammal—the class of animals (including humans) that can help control their own body temperature instead of depending on outside heat or cold, have a backbone, usually have hair, and nourish their young with mother's milk.

Migrate—to travel regularly from one place to another.

Nocturnal—active at night.

Overwinter—to stay in one location throughout the winter.

Ozone layer—the upper atmosphere level of oxygen that helps protect the earth from the sun's ultraviolet rays.

Parasites—animals that live at the cost of other animals, though generally not killing the host animals, at least not immediately.

Reptile—generally an animal that has dry, scaly skin, lays shelled eggs, and depends on outside temperatures for warmth.

Species—a group of individual animals (or plants) that are the same kind of animal (or plant) and can breed and produce young.

Subspecies—a group within a species that is different from the rest of the group, but still the same basic type of animal (or plant).

Threatened species—a species of animal (or plant) that may soon be in danger of becoming extinct in all or a large part of the areas in which it lives.

Ultraviolet radiation—invisible sun rays that can cause sunburn and skin cancer.

FOR FURTHER READING

Bolgiano, Chris. "Unearthing Salamander Secrets." *Defenders* 64. September/October (1989): 12–19.

Douglas, Carole. "A Corridor in Peril." *Wilderness* 53. Winter (1989): 32–37.

Liptak, Karen. *Saving Our Wetlands and Their Wildlife.* New York: Franklin Watts, 1991.

Lowe, David W., John R. Matthews, and Charles J. Moseley, eds. *The Official World Wildlife Fund Guide to Endangered Species of North America,* 2 vols. Washington, D.C.: Beacham Publishing, Inc., 1990.

Milstein, Michael. "Unlikely Harbringers." *National Parks* 64. July/August (1990): 19–24. (Salamanders & other amphibians)

Nash, Stephen. "The Songbird Connection." *National Parks* 64. July/August (1990): 22–27.

Nilsson, Greta. *The Endangered Species Handbook.* Washington, D.C.: The Animal Welfare Institute, 1983.

Steele, Philip. *Extinct Birds: And Those in Danger of Extinction.* New York: Franklin Watts, 1991.

Steele, Philip. *Extinct Reptiles: And Those in Danger of Extinction.* New York: Franklin Watts, 1991.

Sullivan, Sharon. "Guarding the Monarch's Kingdom." *International Wildlife* 17. November/December (1987) 4–10.

Urquhart, Fred A. *The Monarch Butterfly: International Traveler.* Chicago: Nelson Hall, 1987.

Wille, Chris. "Mystery of the Missing Migrants." *Audubon* 92. May (1990) 80–85.

CONSERVATION ORGANIZATIONS YOU CAN CONTACT

Entomological Society of America,9301 Annapolis Road, Lanham, MD 20706-3115, Attention: Dr. Douglas Sutherland, Chairman, ESA National Insect Subcommittee. As for information on the monarch butterfly national insect project.

The Izzak Walton League of America, 1401 Wilson Blvd., Level B, Arlington, VA 22209. Ask about ordering the *SOS (Save Our Streams) Activities for Kids* guide.

Kids Against Pollution, Tenakill School, 275 High Street, Closter, NJ 07624.

National Audubon Society, 950 Third Avenue, New York, NY 10022.

National Wildlife Federation, 1400 Sixteenth Street, NW, Washington, DC 20036-2266

The Nature Conservancy, 1815 N. Lynn Street, Arlington, VA 22209. For information about how individuals or groups can adopt acres of rainforest habitat, write to the Adopt-an-Acre Program at the above address.

The Sierra Club, 730 Polk Street, San Francisco, CA 94109.

The Xerces Society, 10 Southwest Ash Street, Portland OR 97204. This organization works to conserve insects and other invertebrates, including butterflies.

World Wildlife Fund, 1250 24 St., NW, Washington DC 20037

You can find addresses for many other conservation organizations, including federal and state agencies, in the *Conservation Directory*, which is published yearly by the National Wildlife Federation.

INDEX

ABOUT THE AUTHOR

Geraldine Marshall Gutfreund has a degree in zoology from the University of Kentucky. She writes both fiction and nonfiction about both real and imaginary animals. She is also the author of *Animals Have Cousins Too* (Franklin Watts).

Ms. Gutfreund lives with her husband, Mark, daughters, Audrey and Rachel, and dachshund, Newton, near Cincinnati, Ohio, between the villages of Mount Healthy and Greenhills, in a house that backs up to the woods. She loves sharing the land with salamanders, garter snakes, butterflies, and songbirds, but no jaguarundis have yet come to visit.